Shakespeare
COUNTRY

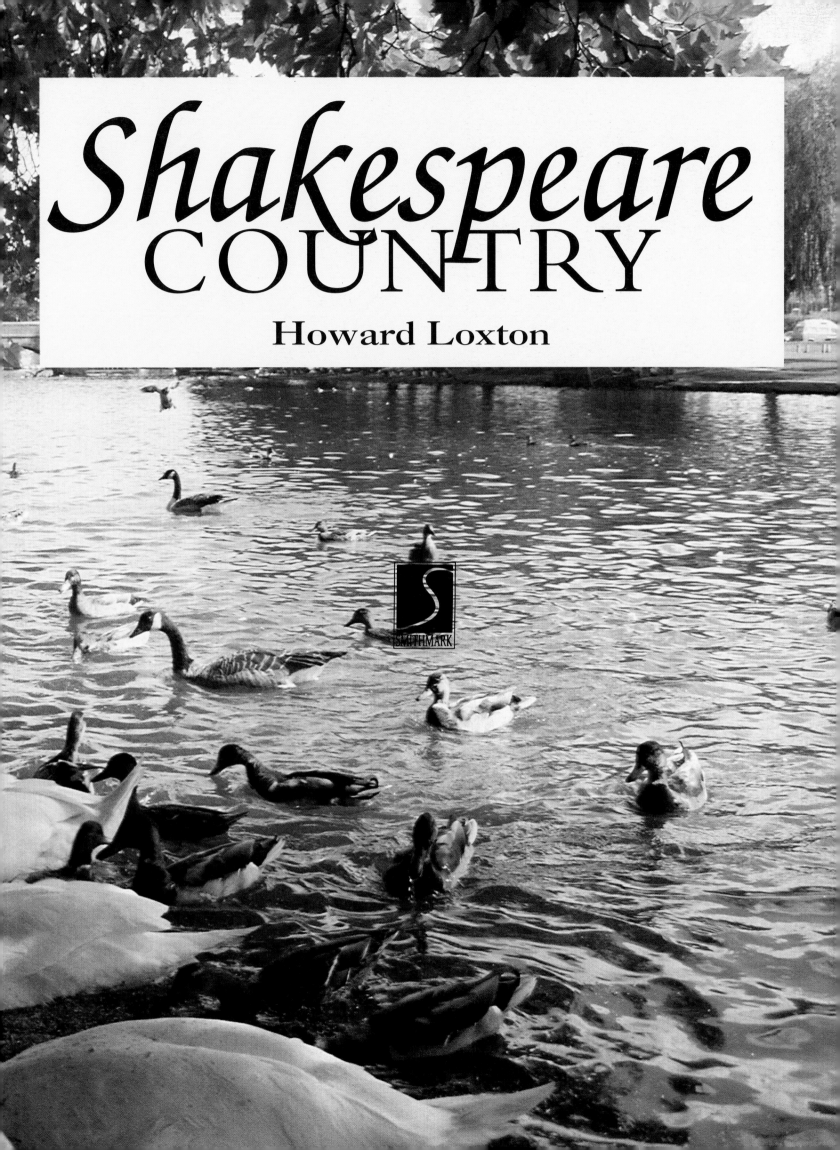

Shakespeare
COUNTRY

Howard Loxton

PHOTOGRAPHIC ACKNOWLEDGEMENTS
Jacket front cover main picture:
Comstock Photo Library
Jacket front cover black and white insert:
Hulton Deutsch Collection
Jacket back cover:
A.F. Kersting

Inside pages:
Comstock Photo Library
39 top, bottom, 40, 41, 64 bottom, 79 top,
(Simon McBride) 17 bottom, 31 top, 34 bottom, 57 top, bottom, 67, 68 top,
79 bottom.

Edifice 43 top, 47.

Derek Forss Photography
4-5, 23, 29 bottom, 38 bottom, 42, 68 bottom.

Hulton Deutsch Collection 7.

Jarrold Publishing, Photographic Library 15 top, bottom, 22 top, 72.

A.F. Kersting
11, 12-13, 14-15, 20-21, 23, 24-25, 26-27, 28, 29 top, 36, 37, 43 bottom, 44-45, 50, 51, 52, 54, 55, 59, 74, 76.

NMR 77; D. Phillips 63; Royal Shakespeare Trust 58-59.

Stratford-upon-Avon Council 1.

Viewpoint Projects
16, 19, 64 top, 70, 75.

Chris Wright Photography
2-3, 10, 17 top, 18-19, 22 bottom, 30-31, 32-33, 34 top, 38 top, 62, 65,
66, 69, 71, 73, 78, 80.

Malcom Porter
Map on pages 8-9

Page 1: The River Avon and Holy Triniy
Pages 2-3: Swans on the Avon
Right: The River Avon at Stratford.

This edition first published in the United States in 1995 by SMITHMARK
Publishers Inc., 16 East 32nd Street, New York, NY 10016.

SMITHMARK books are available for bulk purchase for sales promotion and
premium use. For details write or call the manager of special sales,
SMITHMARK Publishers, 16 East 32nd Street, New York, NY 10016;
(212) 532 6600.

Produced by: Regency House Publishing Limited
The Grange, Grange Yard, London, SE1 3AG.

ISBN 0-8317-1876-5

Printed in the U.A.E.

10 9 8 7 6 5 4 3 2 1

CONTENTS

INTRODUCTION

OPPOSITE

The portrait of William Shakespeare on the title page of the collected edition of his plays published in 1623. Facing it appear some lines by Ben Jonson:

This figure that thou here seest put,
It was for gentle Shakespeare cut,
Wherein the graver had a strife
With nature to outdo the life.
O, could he but have drawn his wit
As well in brass as he has hit
His face, the print would then surpass
All that was ever writ in brass!
But since he cannot, reader, look
Not on his picture, but his book.

The engraver was Martin Droeshout, son of a Flemish immigrant. He would have been only 15 when Shakespeare died, seven years earlier, so most probably he worked from a drawing by another artist. The head seems large for the body and the doublet is poorly drawn but the book's editors, John Heminges and Henry Condell, were old colleagues of the playwright and they and Jonson must have accepted it as a passable likeness, if not a particularly good one.

'He was not of an age, but for all time.' So wrote fellow poet and dramatist Ben Jonson in a memorial poem included in the 1623 collected edition of Shakespeare's plays and poems published seven years after his death. More than 370 years later that assessment still stands. His plays are given more performances each year than those of any other dramatist. Few would challenge his pre-eminence as a poet – and it is not just in the English-speaking world that his reputation stands so high.

Who was this man who wrote plays for theatres that were themselves an innovation in public entertainment, plays that have survived four centuries of changing fashions in drama and poetry that still moves and thrills? To be absolutely honest we cannot be sure. Jonson calls him 'Sweet Swan of Avon' and this reference, together with a memorial which had already been erected in the chancel of Stratford-upon-Avon parish church, and which makes it clear that the William Shakespeare buried there was a writer, are hardly conclusive evidence to identify Stratford William with the authorship of the plays and poems we now attribute to him.

This Shakespeare's father held public office in Stratford and himself became the owner of one of its grandest houses and of other property in the neighbourhood and in London. But that has not stopped some people from questioning his authorship of the plays and poems or from presenting him as an untutored countryman, a provincial incapable of writing them.

Some claim the plays were really written by Christopher Marlowe, whose *Tamburlaine the Great, Doctor Faustus* and other plays appeared before Shakespeare's own. Marlowe was a fine poet, a worthy rival among those of Shakespeare's time; his apparent employment as a government spy and the strange circumstances of his reported death in a pub brawl have encouraged speculation that this was a strategem to allow him to escape prosecution for atheism and homosexual conduct, but it stretches belief that he could have written for over 20 years from exile or in hiding using Shakespeare as a frontman.

Others suggest the true author of 'Shakespeare's' works was the essayist and statesman Francis Bacon, the contemporary Earl of Oxford, or even Queen Elizabeth I herself. They claim to find coded messages in the plays and other sources by which the poet might be revealing his or her real identify. None can even begin to prove their case and, since his theatrical colleagues and contemporaries celebrated Shakespeare's authorship, it seems perverse to question it.

I grew up only a score of miles away from Stratford. Leaving home early, I would cycle to queue for the cheapest seats at what was then known as the Shakespeare Memorial Theatre and then explore Stratford town, the river and the Warwickshire lanes. To me, there was then no doubt that the plays were by our Shakespeare, the Swan of Avon. The life and countryside of this heartland of England is all there in the plays. It pervades his verse as much as any knowledge of the wider world or the chronicles and classical tales from which he so often drew his plots. You do not have to be local born and bred to have this feeling. It is one that many share who come from different lands.

Yet, if you seek a description of, or direct reference to, a particular local setting in his work you will be hard pressed to find it. There are no passages you can point to and link directly with a precise local scene. The sense of the countryside and country living reveal themelves in a multitude of small observations, and in the choice of metaphors. This particular world has been observed so minutely that it seems to emerge from between the very lines of verse.

Shakespeare's dramatic works are above all linked to performance. The plays progress through action, interaction and incident. His characters report events that occur offstage or respond to their environment in a way which helps the audience understand the action. There is very little of the extended descriptive writing on which a novelist may rely. Even in the long narrative poems *Venus and Adonis* and *The Rape of Lucrece* it is the action and emotional impact of the characters which are paramount.

Actors and directors are continually reinterpreting Shakespeare's plays in an attempt to discover new meaning and relevance for their own time. It is a measure of the greatness of his work that they are able to re-create Shakespeare afresh for each new generation. It is all the more mysterious that the plays still manage to remain so deeply rooted to the time in which they were written.

A knowledge of Elizabethan and Jacobean life, and of the England Shakespeare knew, can add considerably to our understanding of his work. Scholars may spend years in research uncovering a topical political reference, explaining a joke that baffles a modern ear or discovering a meaning that now eludes – and actors must find some way of putting over these subtleties to a modern audience. But for those of less academic bent, an exploration of the land that Shakespeare knew, of

Shakespeare Country will bring them even closer.

Shakespeare's own time was one of tremendous change and, in the four centuries which have since elapsed, London has changed beyond recognition. But in his home town of Stratford-upon-Avon much still survives that he would have known. The coming of the motor car and other 20th-century innovations have accelerated the process of change but, especially in the evening when the busy life of the town is stilled, the theatre-goers are sitting engrossed in his plays and the many day tourists attracted by his fame have gone, it is still possible to feel the centuries roll back.

In the surrounding countryside the cycle of the seasons continues to turn from seedtime to harvest, lambing to sheep-shearing.

Quite apart from its Shakespearean associations this part of England is rich in historic buildings, castles, stately homes, lovely countryside and charming villages, though this book concentrates on those places which Shakespeare could have known.

About Shakespeare's personal life in London and elsewhere there is little known and not much of the Elizabethan city still survives, though a new Globe Theatre now rises on the river bank near where Shakespeare's own theatre stood.

The following pages attempt to trace Shakespeare's steps to fame and fortune and back home again to his latter years in Warwickshire; an armchair journey for the reader and an introductory guide for those wishing to make their own Shakespeare pilgrimage.

Shakespeare COUNTRY

Anne Hathaway's cottage

Worcester • • Stratford

• Oxford

LONDON

Shakespeare's birthplace

ALCESTER

to Worcester

Wixford •

Grafto

Hillsborou

Bidford-on-Avon •

R. Avon

Pebwort

EVESHAM

Vale of Evesham

to Tewkesbury

BROADWAY   Dover

C O T S W O

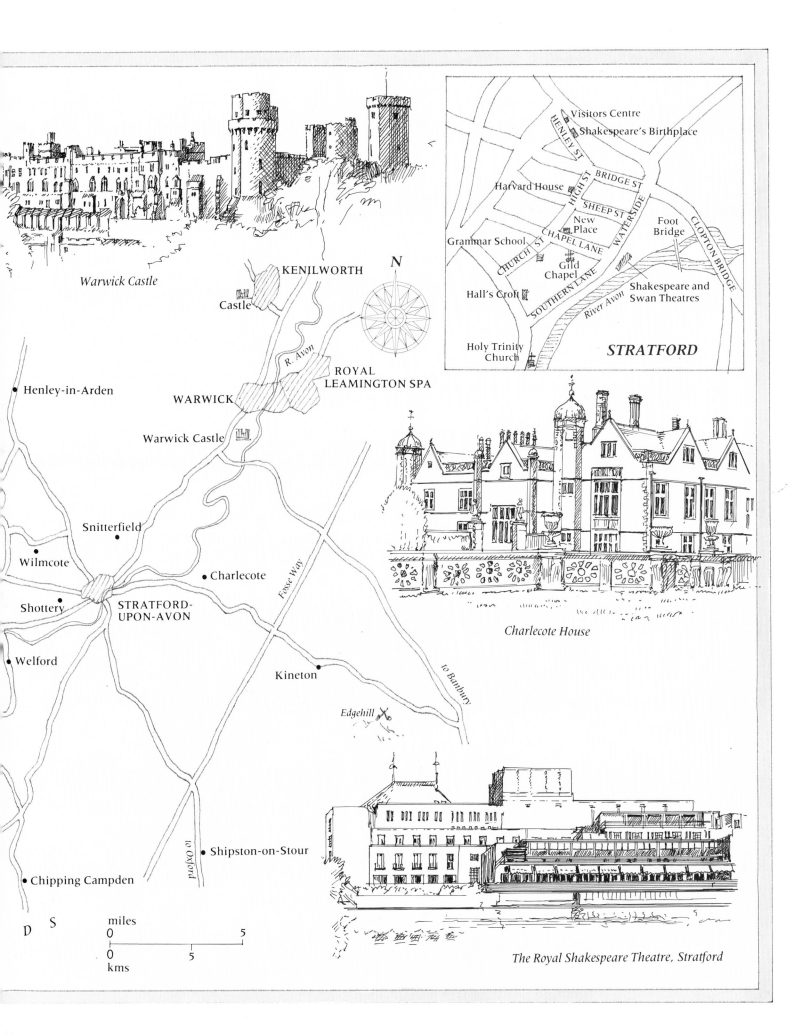

Warwick Castle

KENILWORTH

Castle

N

Visitors Centre

Shakespeare's Birthplace

HENLEY ST

Harvard House

HIGH ST

BRIDGE ST

SHEEP ST

New Place

WATERSIDE

Foot Bridge

CLOPTON BRIDGE

Grammar School

CHAPEL LANE

CHURCH ST

Gild Chapel

Hall's Croft

SOUTHERN LANE

River Avon

Shakespeare and Swan Theatres

Holy Trinity Church

STRATFORD

ROYAL LEAMINGTON SPA

R. Avon

WARWICK

• Henley-in-Arden

Warwick Castle

• Snitterfield

Charlecote House

• Wilmcote

• Charlecote

Fosse Way

Shottery

STRATFORD-UPON-AVON

• Welford

Kineton

to Banbury

Edgehill

to Oxford

• Shipston-on-Stour

• Chipping Campden

D S

miles
0   5

0   5
kms

The Royal Shakespeare Theatre, Stratford

YOUNG WILL AND STRATFORD

The main bedroom in the Henley
Street house, traditionally thought
to be where William Shakespeare
was born, is furnished with
appropriate 16th-century furniture.
The L-shaped metal rod over the
bed is a rushlight holder.

The register of the parish church of Holy Trinity at Stratford-upon-Avon contains an entry written in the ecclesiastical Latin of the day recording the baptism on 26 April 1564 of *Gulielmus filius Johannes Shakspere*, 'William son of John Shakespeare'. His christening is one of the few firm documented facts about him. We have to guess when he was born. Baptisms then took place very soon after birth and this is the reason why William's birthday has traditionally been ascribed to 23 April, St. George's Day, which is appropriate, for one whom England claims to be among her foremost sons, for it is the day of her patron saint. We can assume, though we have no proof, that he was born in his father's house at Henley Street, a substantial dwelling which still survives and is visited by many thousands of tourists each year.

Stratford was a relatively prosperous market town, incorporated as a borough in 1553 and governed by a bailiff (mayor), burgesses and aldermen drawn from its community. Richard I had granted a charter for a weekly market in 1196 and there were annual fairs. John Shakespeare had been elected to the Common Council in 1557, made a Constable (in control of the town watch) in 1558, an Affeeror (responsible for assessing the penalties imposed by the local court) and Chamberlain in 1562. This last post he held for four years, keeping the Borough accounts and supervising welfare and other payments from its coffers.

Shakespeare's birthplace, in Henley Street, Stratford-upon-Avon. In the 16th century this was two properties. Shakespeare's father first occupied the western wing (left) – he was fined in 1553 for having an unauthorized dungheap outside the house. In 1556 he bought the house next door, now the east wing. It is generally thought that this part was then used for his business and the family lived in the other part. Shakespeare was probably born in the main upstairs room. Not long after Shakespeare's death, the eastern part was leased for use as an inn, the 'Maidenhead' or 'Swan and Maidenhead' as it was subsequently known. In later years, the western end became a butcher's shop but the ownership remained with the descendants of Shakespeare's family until the early 18th century. By then, the attic storey gables and dormers had been removed and about 1808 the inn part was fronted with brick. This was the state of the building when it was bought for £3,000, money having been raised by committees set up to preserve the house on behalf of the nation. It was then restored to return it to its earlier condition, basing the work on an etching showing it as it was in 1769. At the same time, adjoining buildings were demolished to reduce the fire risk.

The greater part of the structure was built in the late 15th or early 16th century. A low foundation wall of local stone supports a frame superstructure of oak, which is filled in with wattle and daub. A massive chimney stack gives central support. Most of the internal timbers are in their oiginal positions and the western part of the building retains many of its original exterior timbers too.

Later, when little Will was four, he held the high office of Bailiff.

Will's father had been raised on the family farm at Snitterfield, a village three miles north of Stratford, but moved to Stratford where, by 1552, he had set himself up as a glove-maker in Henley Street. This must have entailed some years of apprenticeship before acceptance to the Craft of Glovers, Whitetawers (dressers of white leather) and Collarmakers. He may have been consciously trying to improve himself in order to make himself a more acceptable suitor for one of the daughters of the landlord of the farm at Snitterfield, Mary Arden.

The Ardens were a family that dated back before the Norman Conquest but Mary's father, Robert, though having the right to the family coat of arms, was a very junior scion. Despite receiving income from his land he had run his own farm at Wilmcote, to the north-east of Stratford. The grander side of the family lived at Park Hall, near Salford Priors in northern Warwickshire and one of them, Edward Arden was sheriff of Warwick in 1575.

When Robert died in 1556, Mary inherited a six-acre farm called Asbies and more than six pounds in cash, a handsome bequest for an eighth child to receive and a welcome dowry for her marriage to John Shakespeare sometime in the following year.

In September their first child, Joan, was christened. She probably died in infancy, since nothing is known of her, and a later daughter was given the same name. Another girl followed in 1562 but she too had died, perhaps of the Plague, which ravaged England before William was born in 1564. Three further sons were born and two daughters, though one lived only to the age of eight.

John Shakespeare dealt in wool, grain and other commodities as well as gloves. He may have bought calves on the hoof and sold their flesh and made use of their leather. A later tradition which makes him a butcher and fancies young Will killing calves while making high flown speeches. Probably this idea had its origin in the later use of part of the Henley Street house as a butcher's shop from the end of the 18th century.

In the early years of John

'Mary Arden's House' at Wilmcote, four miles northwest of Stratford, is reputed to have belonged to Shakespeare's mother's family and to have been her childhood home. A considerable property of timber frame and wattle and daub, it was originally built in Henry VIII's time or earlier but altered in Elizabeth I's reign. It was a working farm until acquired by the Birthplace Trust in 1930 and still has its old barns, a dovecote and a cider-mill. The dovecote is evidence that this was once a manor house for, with the exception of the rector of a parish, no one of lower rank than a squire was permitted to have such a structure.

A detailed inventory was made of Robert Arden's property when he died in 1556 and this was used as a guide to refurnishing it. There are fewer visitors here than to the other properties associated with Shakespeare and, although too neat and polished for a working farm, it is the most successful in recapturing a sense of the past. Across a meadow, the adjoining Glebe Farm has now been arranged to suggest a later, 19th century working farm. Together, these offer an outdoor museum of Warwickshire farming life.

Shakespeare's marriage, his businesses did well and in 1575 he was still adding to his Stratford properties: but by the time William was in his teens things were going wrong. The solid citizen who had held public office for 20 years was missing Council meetings. He was defaulting on his contributions to the cost of the watch, and the fourpence a week which aldermen contributed to poor relief. In 1579 he was forced to mortgage his wife's estate at Asbies and her share in the farm at Snitterfield was sold to a nephew. The Shakespeares were getting into debt. Perhaps John had been neglecting business because he was devoting so much time to civic affairs. It has been suggested that he

The Gild of the Holy Cross was founded in the 13th century and granted a licence to build its chapel in 1269, though most of the present fabric is a later remodelling of the Early English structure. The chancel is early 15th-century, the tower, porch and nave having being completed and paid for by a bequest from Sir Hugh Clopton at the end of the century. Sir Hugh's arms are displayed by an angel in the north doorway: a lion quartering a cross formy fitchy. The Gild was founded to maintain chaplains to pray for the souls of its members, important men and women of the town and county, as an aid to their own welfare, and to support the poor, the school and almshouse. When in 1547, along with other religious foundations, it was suppressed and its properties seized by the Crown, the townsfolk petitioned King Edward VI to make Stratford a borough and to grant it the Gild's properties. The boy king granted their request shortly before his death. The grammar school, like so many refounded in a similar way, thereafter carried his name.

BELOW RIGHT
Stratford Grammar School yard, the pedagogue's house on the right.

may have been crippled by the fines levied on Catholics who failed to attend the services of the reformed English Church but – though relative Edward Arden was a known Catholic, who was beheaded later for involvement in a plot to assassinate Elizabeth – it seems unlikely: it was when John Shakespeare was bailiff that the Roman Catholic features of the Gild Chapel were removed and the carved 'images' defaced. However, he was summoned to Westminster in 1580 (along with many more) to provide sureties that he would maintain the Queen's Peace, and was fined for not turning up. This may bear some relation to missed church attendances. Six years later he was deprived of the office of alderman because 'Mr Shaxpere dothe not come to the Halles when they be warned nor hathe not done of longe tyme'.

What can this tell us about young Will's childhood? He came of yeoman stock, with rather more grand connections, successful and well respected in the community – though misjudged speculation, bad harvests or some other cause tightened the purse-strings while the family grew bigger. We cannot even be sure that he was reared at home: he could have been sent off to earn his keep and share a tutor in one of the great houses, perhaps one connected to the Arden family. However, Stratford had its own grammar school, originally founded by the Gild of the Holy Cross and reconstituted under Edward VI. That is where he most likely gained the 'small Latin and less Greek' which Ben

Jonson accords him, to add to the letters learned at his mother's knee and probably at a 'petty school' which accepted pupils from the age of seven years.

The alphabet would have been conned from a hornbook, originally a framed sheet with the letters written out protected by a thin layer of cattle horn. Then he would have learned to read and write, though Elizabethan spelling tended to be variable – just look at the many different spellings of Shakespeare's name in various documents – an incentive perhaps to the punning which was so popular in those times.

The main purpose of a grammar school was to provide a grounding in Latin grammar. It was just over a century since Caxton had published the

Inside the Gild Chapel, where young William Shakespeare, as a pupil of the school, would have attended daily worship. He would not have seen the Doomsday painting which can still be discerned upon the chancel arch, depicting the saved on the right and the damned on the left being boiled in cauldrons or cast into the flames by devils. Seen as papist images, they would have been whitewashed over shortly before his birth.

first printed book in English, and 40 years since Henry VIII had approved an English translation of the Bible and the issue of the Book of Common Prayer. This put English church services into the vernacular, but Latin was still the international language of intellectual and scientific publication.

The schoolmaster at the Stratford grammar school when William was a pupil was a Welshman called Thomas Jenkins and it is possible that he was later re-invented as Sir Hugh Evans in *The Merry Wives of Windsor*. This pleasantly comic Welsh schoolmaster, called Sir because he has a bachelor's degree from the university not because he is a knight, even has a scene where he tests a lad (appropriately called William) on his Latin declensions.

Although William would not have aspired to the academic standards of some of his contemporaries, men like Ben Jonson or Christopher Marlowe, his schoolboy level was probably at least as good as the standards of a modern university degree in classical languages. At school he would have made his first acquaintance with the classics, including the works of Ovid, Virgil, Horace, Caesar and Plutarch, though they were probably used more as exercises for translating Latin into English and vice versa, guides to Latin grammar rather than literature to be read for its own sake. He would also have studied the rules of rhetoric and the conventions of formal letter writing

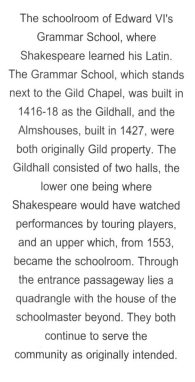

The schoolroom of Edward VI's Grammar School, where Shakespeare learned his Latin. The Grammar School, which stands next to the Gild Chapel, was built in 1416-18 as the Gildhall, and the Almshouses, built in 1427, were both originally Gild property. The Gildhall consisted of two halls, the lower one being where Shakespeare would have watched performances by touring players, and an upper which, from 1553, became the schoolroom. Through the entrance passageway lies a quadrangle with the house of the schoolmaster beyond. They both continue to serve the community as originally intended.

and oratory.

Of the Latin texts he was set he probably read the tragedies of Seneca and the comedies of Terence and Plautus (from which he was later to borrow some of his plots). At the universities and at some schools students were now putting on performances of these ancient Roman plays. In 1560, Queen Elizabeth had decreed that every Christmas the scholars of Westminster should perform a Latin play 'that the young may spend Christmas with greater benefit and become better acquainted with proper action and pronunciation'. You may well like to fancy Will as a schoolboy actor declaiming in Latin before family and friends.

They were not the only plays to see. The performance of the religious miracle and mystery plays by members of craft guilds had been forbidden when Elizabeth I came to the throne, but references in his plays to ways of playing Herod, and to the character personifying Vice in the morality plays, suggest Shakespeare was familiar with them and may have seen some of them before they disappeared completely. England's first playhouse was not opened in London until he was 12 years old, but there were already well established groups of touring actors who sometimes came to Stratford. There were at least a dozen visits by various companies during Shakespeare's boyhood and teens – his father, when he was

Mason's Court, in Rother Street, is one of the oldest of Stratford's houses. When first built, in the 15th century, the timber frame would have been filled with panels of wattle and daub, later replaced by the brick nogging seen today. Originally, this group of houses was a single house consisting of a hall in the middle, open from ground to roof, flanked by wings with upper storeys. The wings extend to the rear to enclose a small courtyard, now reached by a covered passage from the street.

A woodcut from a contemporary pamphlet depicting a water pageant given for Elizabeth I at Elvetham in 1591. It was the kind of entertainment which would have been presented at Kenilworth and whose mermaids, fireworks and romantic homage to the Virgin Queen may have suggested Oberon's recollection in *A Midsummer Night's Dream*:

... Thou rememb'rest
Since once I sat upon a
promontary,
And heard a mermaid on a
dolphin's back,
Uttering such dulcet and
harmonious breath,
That the rude sea grew
civil at her song;
And certain stars shot
madly from their spheres,
To hear the sea-maid's
music?...
That very time I saw, but
thou couldst not,
Flying between the cold
moon and the earth,
Cupid, all armed: a certain
aim he took
At a fair vestal, throned by
the west;
And loosed his love-shaft
smartly from his bow,
As it should pierce a
hundred thousand hearts ...

Chamberlain, had been responsible for paying their fees for performing in the Guildhall.

In the summer of 1575, Queen Elizabeth made her fourth visit to Kenilworth Castle, which she had given as a gift to her favourite, the Earl of Leicester. There he mounted elaborate entertainments for her diversion. Kenilworth is only 10 miles or so from Stratford and 11-year-old Will may have managed to get to see something of the water pageants and other extravagant spectacles.

On foot or by horseback – and with farming uncles on both sides of the family Will must surely have had a

Kenilworth Castle. The solid Norman keep was built for Henry II and the curtain walls and towers date from about 1210. John of Gaunt gave it to his son, who became Henry IV, and it remained a royal castle until 1563 when Elizabeth I gave it to her favourite, Robert Dudley, a year before creating him Earl of Leicester. He added Leycester's Buildings and the gatehouse. In 1575, Elizabeth came for a 12-day visit and Leicester laid on lavish entertainments with which to amuse her.

mount available to him – there were many other places of interest within easy reach. Nearer to home was the county town of Warwick, with the great castle of the Earls of Warwick, and further on in the same direction, Coventry. North, beyond the family farms towards the Arden mansion lay the Forest of Arden, then stretching in a band some ten miles wide for about 20 miles. South, lay the rich arable lands then known as the Feldon and the rolling hills of the Cotswolds, whose little towns and villages had grown rich from the medieval wool trade. The Avon flowed down through the Vale of Evesham, rich in orchards, to Tewkes-

bury, while to the west, on the River Severn, lay the city of Worcester, seat of the diocese of which Stratford was part.

Did William go 'unwillingly to school?' Schoolboys had a long and exhausting day which began at seven in the morning (six in summer) and went on until five in the afternoon. There was a break for breakfast at about nine and another of two hours in the middle of the day. There were two half-days off a week and Sundays, and 40 days of holiday each year. Was Shakespeare made to spend those half-days and holidays helping with the family business, especially when it was not not doing well, or was he allowed to play with his

The little market town of Henley-in Arden, a few miles north of Stratford. Long known as 'leafy Warwickshire', the county has seen a steady reduction in its forests. In Shakespeare's time, the Forest of Arden was deep woodland, thinly studded with pastoral settlements, though already beginning to give way to agriculture. On the other side of the Avon across to Edgehill were the arable lands of the Feldon, the rich granary which fed Bristol and the country to the southwest with corn shipped down the Avon.

OPPOSITE PAGE
The Feldon from Edgehill, site of the first battle of the English Civil War in 1642. During Shakespeare's time there was an increasing demand for wood from the ironworks developing to the north of Stratford, in Birmingham and Staffordshire, and the Forest of Arden lost many of its trees, increasing the amount of arable land. By the end of the century the Forest had almost disappeared and most of the Feldon had been given over to grass, reducing the population of many villages to only a few shepherds.

Sheep grazing on the edge of the Cotswolds near Ilmington. This part of England (like parts of East Anglia) was an area which contributed much of the wool production which provided medieval England with its major exports, wool and woollen cloth. The wealth it brought built many fine churches in the downs nestling in and around the Cotswolds. The characteristic dry-stone walling provided protection from the wind but they also broke up the great sheep runs into fields when Cotswold farming began to shift to agriculture in the 18th century.

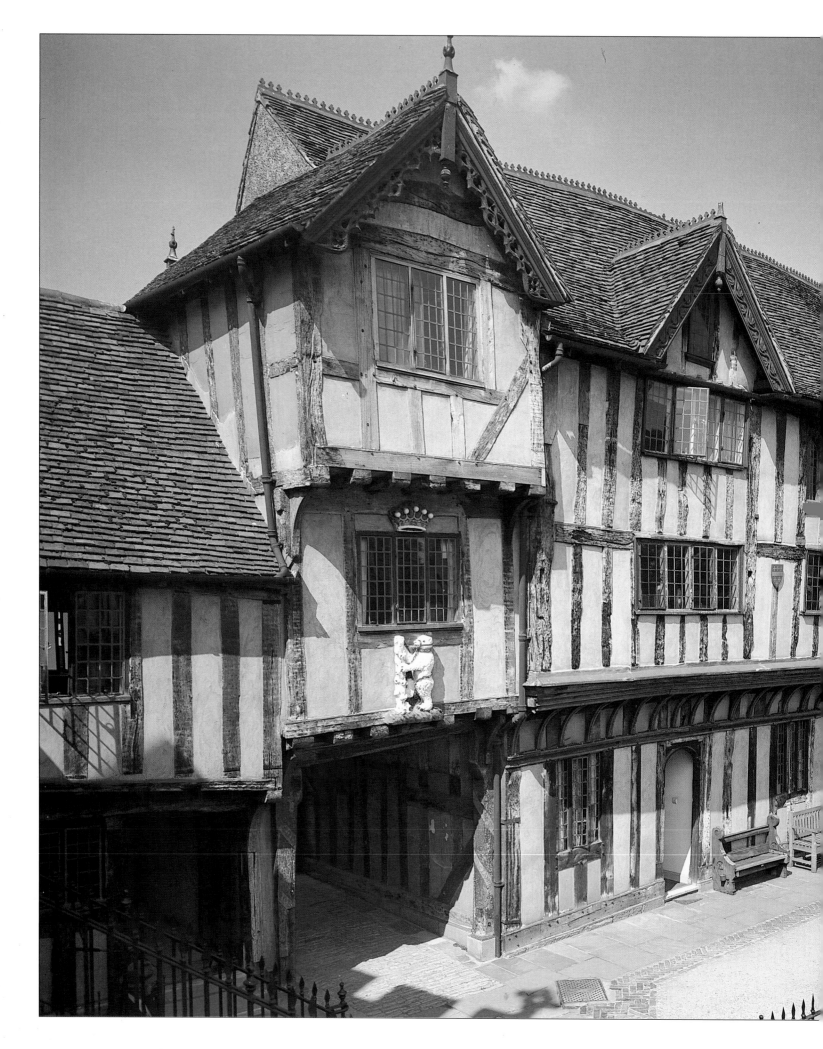

fellows, enjoy the river and roam the surrounding countryside? He certainly seems to have become well acquainted with flowers, birds and country pursuits and had a naturalist's eye for such detail as the little pattern of red spots that appear within the petals of a cowslip for he mentions them in his plays. Was he a bookish lad? We do not know what books, if any, he may have had at home but the local rector is known to have had a good collection and to have been prepared to lend them to readers: there were probably other available sources even if there was no money to buy his own. Did he try his hand at writing himself, perhaps in imitation of the classical writers whose plots he later made use of in some of his plays.

Sadly, we can only make conjectures. When he left school, probably at 16, we have no idea whether he attempted to learn a trade or how he earned his living. Hard facts start to appear in 1582 when William was 18. There is an entry in the register of the Worcester Diocese that on 27 November, a licence was issued for the marriage of 'Wm Shaxpere et Anna Whateley de Temple Grafton'. That seems quite straightforward except that next day, two Shottery farmers, Fulk Sandells and John Richardson, bound

Lord Leycester's Hospital. Beside the ancient West Gate in Warwick is a range of timbered buildings dating from the end of the 15th or beginning of the 16th centuries. Until the dissolution of the monasteries, they belonged to three medieval guilds, those of Holy Trinity, St. George and the Blessed Virgin, and for a time after 1546 housed the grammar school. But in 1571, they became the property of the Queen's favourite, Robert Dudley, Earl of Leicester. He converted them into a hospital (or asylum) for 12 men, preferably old soldiers from Warwickshire or Gloucestershire and tenants or servants of the founder, who were precluded from having an income of more than five pounds a year on admission. They wore a uniform of a cap and a blue gown with a badge consisting of Dudley's bear and ragged staff crest, presented by Queen Elizabeth. Modern residents of Lord Leycester's Hospital can still be seen wearing it when attending church on Sundays.

Warwick Castle, set on the Avon a few miles above Stratford, was the seat of the warlike Earls of Warwick. An early Norman castle was destroyed in 1264. Most of the old fortifications date from the 14th and 15th centuries, though later domestic buildings and fine gardens have made this as much a stately home as a castle. Queen Elizabeth came here in 1572, when Shakespeare was eight years old. After watching folk-dances in the courtyard she was entertained by a grand fireworks display culminating in a flying dragon of exploding squibs which nearly set the town on fire! In the decades that followed, the castle fell into decay but when James I made a present of it to Fulke Greville, in 1604, the new owner began an expensive restoration.

themselves in a document in the same diocesan records to act as sureties for the legality of a marriage between 'Willm Shagspere' and an 'Anne Hathwey'.

Certainly William Shakespeare did marry Anne Hathaway (as we now spell their names) and she bore him a daughter who was christened Susanna in the parish church at Stratford less than six months later. What was going on? Was Shakespeare in a hurry to marry one girl before the family of another woman, whom he had got with child, could force a shotgun wedding? The Anne he did marry was already 26, eight years his senior, and living with her stepmother and half-brothers and probably eager to get away from them. Had she encouraged a lusty young man in the hope of conceiving so that he would be duty bound to marry her?

The story may be much simpler, merely a careless clerk and makeshift spelling of both names. There was some earlier incident on 26 November involv-

Castle Street Passage, Warwick, and the parish church of St. Mary, built by the Earls of Warwick. The nave and tower were restored after damage in the fire of 1694 which destroyed much of the town.

The beautiful Beauchamp Chapel in St. Mary's, Warwick, was built in fulfilment of the will of Richard Beauchamp, the fifth Earl, whose father and grandfather had built the original church. This was the Earl of Warwick who was tutor to Henry VI and soldier in the Hundred Years War and who appears not only in Shakespeare's Henry VI Part I but also in George Bernard Shaw's St. Joan. In the centre of the chapel is his magnificent gilded bronze effigy reclined on a marble tomb chest bearing reliefs of mourners familiar from Shakespeare's histories such as Stafford and Richard Neville, the 'Kingmaker' Earl of Warwick. Here, too, is the ornate tomb of Robert Dudley, Earl of Leicester and his wife and those of his sons: Robert, died aged three and his tiny suit of armour can be seen in the castle. His brother, Ambrose, succeeded as Earl of Warwick.

Worcester Cathedral, dedicated to Christ and the Blessed Virgin, is set on the banks of the River Severn. The special licence for Shakespeare's wedding was issued here.

ing a William Whately which may have been responsible for the error. Perhaps it had taken that long for the pregnancy to be sufficiently noticeable to convince the father. Since the Church discouraged the celebration of marriages during Advent and Christmastide, and charged more for a special licence, there was good financial reason to get it solemnized before the end of the month.

The marriage may not even have been contracted under duress but, whether it was or not, the families may

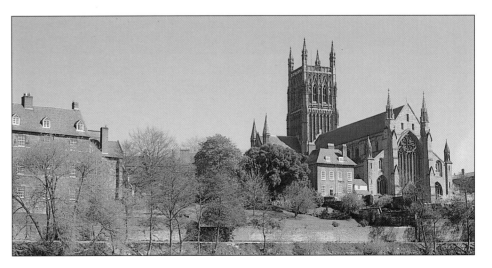

Hewland's Farm, at Shottery, a mile west of Stratford, is more popularly known as Anne Hathaway's Cottage. The Hathaway family certainly lived here. John Hathaway was a tenant of the manor in 1543 and his son and grandson Richard, Anne's father, succeeded him, so that Anne (or Agnes, as she was referred to in her father's will) grew up here. Her brother, Bartholomew, bought the house in 1610 for £200 and it stayed in the family until 1838, when it was divided into three cottages. 'Cottage' is an 18th-century misnomer used to describe the romantic prettiness of the building; it was a substantial timber-framed yeoman-farmer's dwelling of 12 rooms, with a thatched roof. In the year before William's birth, John Shakespeare stood surety for Richard Hathaway to the tune of £19; the families had enjoyed links of friendship long before their children became involved with each other.

The Avon in winter, with Holy Trinity
where Shakespeare's children were
all christened.

When icicles hang on the wall,
And Dick the shepherd blows his nail,
And Tom bears logs into the hall,
And milk comes frozen home in pail;

When blood is nipped, and ways be foul,
Then nightly sings the staring owl:
Tu-whit, tu-whoo! - a merry note,
While greasy Joan doth keel the pot.

When all aloud the wind doth blow,
And coughing drowns the parson's saw,
And birds sit brooding in the snow,
And Marian's nose looks red amd raw;

When roasted crabs hiss in the bowl,
Then nightly sings the staring owl:
Tu-whit, tu-whoo! - a merry note,
While greasy Joan doth keel the pot.

Love's Labour's Lost Act 5, Scene 2

33

use of terms from a wide variety of trades and professions in his plays has prompted suggestions that he might have worked as a schoolteacher, a lawyer, a soldier, a sailor or at any of the many occupations to which allusion can be found. The concensus of opinion is that he did not stay long in Stratford, but when or why he left must once again be the subject of conjecture.

One oft-told local story is that he fled Stratford having being caught poaching deer on the estate of Sir Thomas Lucy at nearby Charlcote. Maybe he was tempted to go to London by news of how well fellow Stratfordian Richard Field was doing. Richard was

Chipping Camden. The tall, airy parish church of St. James, flooded with light from its great windows, was built from the profits of the wool trade.

have wished to avoid attracting unnecessary attention by arranging it to take place at Temple Grafton, some way further west of Stratford than Shottery. Even so, no entry for the marriage has been found there.

The newly-weds were likely to have made their home with the Shakespeare family in Henley Street. Little Susanna was less than a year old when Anne became pregnant again, giving birth to twins in February 1585. They were christened Hamnet and Judith. William was not yet 21, but these three were to be his only children, legitimate ones at least. Were two pregnancies in quick succession followed by marital abstinence or paternal absence? It is difficult to imagine youthful libido fading so quickly.

We do not know what William did to support his family. The knowledgeable apprenticed to a London printer and later married his master's widow.

Or did Shakespeare throw his lot in with a troupe of actors? Stratford was visited by several companies in the period when he might have joined them: The Earl of Worcester's Men, for instance, whose principal player was the young Edward Alleyn, two years William's junior, and The Queen's Men, the most successful company of the decade, led by comedians Richard Tarlton and William Kemp.

One of The Queen's Men was killed just before their visit in 1587; did William take his place, packing his bags and departing with them? It is more than likely that Shakespeare became an actor before he became a playwright and it is certain that a play by Shakespeare, though not necessarily entirely his own work, was successful in London in 1590-1, sufficiently so for an older, once popular rival to disparage him in a pamphlet published in 1592.

Whether he set off across Clopton Bridge and directly to London, or arrived at the capital after travels elsewhere, the journey between London and Stratford was likely to have occurred regularly in later years. The route would have taken him through Oxford where it has been claimed he was a regular visitor at the Crown Inn.

The Woolstapler's Hall, in the main street of Chipping Camden, was built eleven years after Shakespeare's death at the expense of Sir Baptist Hicks who, with his wife, is carved in effigy in grey and white stone in St. James's Church. Chipping comes from the Anglo-Saxon *caepen*, meaning market, and the shelter of cool stone was intended for the sale of local butter, cheese and poultry. This delightful Cotswold town, thriving centre of the wool trade, is within easy reach of Stratford.

Charlecote House, four miles out from Stratford to the west, was the seat of the Lucy family. There is an old tradition that Shakespeare left Stratford as a young man to flee the wrath of Sir Thomas Lucy after being caught on the baronet's land poaching deer. It is thought that he was either whipped by the keepers or imprisoned by Sir Thomas himself – for he was also a magistrate. Shakespeare supposedly wrote a scurrilous doggerel with Sir Thomas as its subject and was forced to flee to escape further retribution. It has been suggested, in contradiction of the tale, that Shakespeare would have had great difficulty carrying a dead deer back to Stratford unobserved; but of course he may have had local accomplices. The story collapses somewhat, for at that time the Charlecote estate had not yet been enclosed and there were no deer to be poached. It does seem, however, that there are echoes of Sir Thomas in the plays: Justice Shallow in The Merry Wives of Windsor is given a coat-of-arms of a dozen white luces (the Lucy arms had three); but Shakespeare scholar Dr. Leslie Hotson has come up with another candidate for caricature in a London magistrate, William Gardiner, with whom Shakespeare had a quarrel of long standing and whose arms bore the Lucy emblems in its quartering.

INSET

Charlcote Park certainly has its deer today, an attractive addition to the fine landscaping surrounding the Elizabethan mansion, which retains much of the original 16th-century structure despite 19th-century additions and restorations.

Clopton Bridge, the beginning of the road to Oxford or Banbury and then on to London. Stratford had had a wooden bridge across the river at least from the 13th century. This handsome stone bridge was built by Sir Hugh Clopton in 1490. Sir Hugh, younger son of a local landowning family had become a successful London mercer – he was Mayor of London the following year – and was a generous benefactor to his home town.

At one time, travellers would have had to pay a toll to cross it. It is still Stratford's highway crossing, although in 1651 one of its 14 arches was rebuilt after being blown up in the Civil War as a defensive measure. The nearby pedestrian bridge was built in 1823 to carry a horse-drawn tramway from Moreton-in-Marsh, linking it with the river and canal at Stratford. This was last used about 1881; one of the old wagons can be seen at the end of the bridge.

The road through Banbury offers an alternative route to and from London. Banbury is famous for a very special kind of cake consisting of a pastry base filled with currants, raisins and candied peel and topped with a criss-cross pattern; this is no doubt an allusion to the Cross mentioned in the nursery rhyme:

Ride a cock-horse
To Banbury Cross
To see a fine lady
On a white horse.
Rings on her fingers
And bells on her toes,
She shall have music
Wherever she goes.

Shakespeare may have seen the Cross which was smashed by Puritans in the 17th century but replaced by another in the 19th century.

Oxford has long been a seat of learning. The oldest college, University College, was founded in 1249, though the oldest college building is St. Edmund's Hall, built later in the century. According to John Aubrey, 'Mr. William Shakespeare was wont to goe into Warwickshire once a yeare' and for that annual visit he travelled via Oxford where he frequently stayed at the Crown Inn. The hostess there was Mistress Davenant,'a very beautiful woman & of a very good witt and of conversation extremely agreeable'. Her son, William Davenant (knighted in 1643 for his service to the Royalist cause) who did much to bring theatre back to London after it had been banned by the Puritans, claimed that Shakespeare was his natural father.

THE GLOBE-TROTTER

The Rialto Bridge, Venice. This inevitably springs to mind whenever the city is mentioned, even if one has never visited Venice. When he wrote *The Merchant of Venice*, Shakespeare seemed to be just as familiar with the Jewish ghetto.

Venice makes a particularly appropriate setting for a play hinging on the development of capitalism, which was then becoming established.

Shakespeare sets his plays in locations which range from familiar English places to such exotic lands as Egypt and the countries of the Levant. *Love's Labour's Lost* is set in Navarre, a kingdom straddling the Pyrenees, the northern part of which had become part of France in the decade before the play was written. *All's Well that Ends Well* is set in southern France and *As You Like It* further north in the Ardennes. *The Taming of the Shrew* is largely set in Padua, *Romeo and Juliet* in Verona and *Two Gentleman of Verona* in Milan. *Much Ado About Nothing* takes place in Sicily, *A Winter's Tale* in Sicily and Bohemia, *Othello* in

Cyprus and *The Tempest* on an island in the Mediterranean somewhere between Naples and Tunis. *Twelfth Night* is set in Illyria on the Dalmatian coast and the action of *Pericles, Prince of Tyre* is set all around the eastern Mediterranean. *Macbeth* is set in Scotland, and *Hamlet* in Denmark while *Measure for Measure* takes place in Vienna, and *A Midsummer Night's Dream* and *Timon of Athens* in Athens. Then there are all the plays based on Greek and Roman history which have a multitude of locations from Rome to Alexandria and Troy, Actium and Philippi while the English histories are set right across Britain from the Welsh coast to the

This ancient building in Verona attracts tourists wishing to see 'Juliet's balcony'. There already existed versions of the story in Italian, French and English before Shakespeare wrote his play *Romeo and Juliet*. They were thus fictional characters of long standing rather than historical figures. Shakespeare probably worked mainly from a poem published in 1562 by Arthur Brooke and was certainly unlikely to have been inspired by a visit to Verona! This balcony gained its name much later from the tourist trade.

Wash, from Northumberland to Dover and across to France.

There have been people who claim this geographical knowledge as evidence that Shakespeare had travelled widely, somewhat contradicted by his descriptions of the French Ardennes and the woods of Theseus's Athens. They have a strong English feel and manage to retain an uncanny resemblance to the Warwickshire Forest of Arden. While in the geography of his imagination, land-locked Bohemia acquires a sea coast! The locations in his plays are intended as glamorous settings for his characters, fitting their needs, rather than the other way around. What tourists now see as Juliet's balcony is a testament to the power of Shakespeare's imagination which has impressed itself upon their own. His choice of location was secondary to the stories that he was adapting – for most of his plots had been developed from, or are a palimpsest of stories surviving from earlier times. The setting of a famous city or distant land might have added an aura of romance and exoticism to a plot but was not in a strict sense vital to it.

Yet that is not to say that Shakespeare did not travel. He could, conceivably, have become a seaman and sailed around the Mediterranean or have

soldiered in Europe before achieving success as a playwright.

He may also have travelled as an actor. In 1591 the will of a Lancashire gentleman, Alexander Houghton, commends a player in his household called William Shakeshafte to Sir Thomas Hesketh, a man known to have connections with Lord Strange who was patron of a company of actors. Shakeshafte is one of the forms the family name is known to have taken. Could this be evidence of a visit by Stratford William to the North before obtaining introduction to a London company? He may even have joined the household in some other capacity, maybe as a tutor.

The gossipy writings of the 17th-century antiquarian and gossip John Aubrey are not known for their reliability but he declared quite categorically of Shakespeare 'Though as Ben Jonson sayes of him, that he had but little Latine and lesse Greek, he understood Latine pretty well: for he had been in his younger yeares a Schoolmaster in the Countrey'. Aubrey claims to have received this information from the son of Christopher Beeston, one of Shakespeare's fellow actors. He could well have been an usher, the assistant

The Abbey and ancient town of Tewkesbury. It stands south of Worcester where the Rivers Avon and Severn join, still dominated by the Norman tower of its famous abbey. It was an important place in the middle ages. Here, in 1471, one of the great battles of the Wars of the Roses took place: the Yorkists were routing Queen Margaret's Lancastrian forces when the Prince of Wales was killed near the Abbey, struck down by a blow from the Yorkist Edward IV's gauntlet. Shakespeare's version of the incident in *Henry VI Part III (The True Tragedy of Richard, Duke of York and the Good King Henry the Sixth)* has the prince stabbed by all three Yorkist brothers, Edward, George and Richard.

teacher in a grammar school.

Although the acting companies with which Shakespeare came to be associated in the years of his success are not recorded as readily embarking on tours overseas, he could have travelled in this capacity, for English companies *did* perform on the Continent, in English: The Queen's Men had been on tour in Europe in 1586, their bookings including peformances for the King of Denmark and the Duke of Saxony. In 1598 another English company hired the principal theatre in Paris: English acting was already famous abroad, overseas visitors remarking favourably on its quality after their visits to the London theatres. Had Shakespeare, like *Hamlet*'s travelling players, actually been to Elsinore?

However, Shakespeare's knowledge of foreign names and places did not require first-hand experience any more than he would have had to have worked as a lawyer or been a king to write about litigation or the burdens of a crown. He seems to have read widely and must surely have applied a writer's careful ear, not only to the latest news and gossip, but to craftsmen and members of the professions when they were 'talking shop'. He would have taken mental notes when consulting his doctor, or when he sat in taverns, avidly engrossed in the yarns of soldiers and seamen newly returned to London. He would have absorbed many a traveller's tales from merchants, musicians and actors. He was well able to improve his knowledge from conversing

Shakespeare Cliff, part of the white Cliffs of Dover. In *King Lear* the blind Duke of Gloucester asks to be led to the cliff's edge to throw himself over it. His companion (his son Edgar though he does not know it) thwarts his attempt at suicide by taking him to a small declivity and describing it as though it were the real cliff:

Come on, sir; here's the place. Stand still. How fearful

And dizzy 'tis, to cast one's eyes so low!

The crows and choughs, that wing the midway air

Show scarce so gross as beetles. Halfway down

Hangs one that gathers samphire, dreadful trade!

Methinks, he seems no bigger than his head:

The fishermen, that walk upon the beach,

Appear like mice; and yon tall anchoring barque,

Diminished to her cock; her cock a buoy

Almost too small for sight. The murmuring surge,

That on th'unnumbered idle pebbles chafes,

Cannot be heard so high. I'll look no more,

Lest my brain turn, and the deficient sight

Topple down headlong.

Act 4, Scene 6

with colleagues, such as Ben Jonson, who had had a university education. He had friends among the nobility who may have spoken of state affairs or military campaigns, and among their households were men such as John Florio, the Earl of Southampton's secretary, a former professor of languages at Oxford, translator from the French and Italian languages.

Small details can go a long way to conjure up an atmosphere , and it helps if they are easily recognized by the audience. Italianate names, mention of ducats and 'the Rialto', and a single reference to a gondola are the only local colour in *The Merchant of Venice* – and even that is more than will be found in many of the plays. In *A Midsummer Night's Dream,*

Theseus, Duke of Athens, has a bride and courtiers with classical names and the occasional reference to the Greek hero's past history is even thrown in, but the action seems to take place in a very English setting. A prospective visitor to Greece is therefore most unlikely to seek historical information about Theseus by consulting Shakespeare's play. Nevertheless, Shakespeare's characters have such a powerful hold on the imagination that visitors to Elsinore or Verona find the names of Hamlet and Ophelia, Romeo and Juliet springing immediately to mind as though they were once the true inhabitants of the place.

LONDON AND THE THEATRE

O for a muse of fire, that
would ascend
The brightest heaven of
invention:
A kingdom for a stage,
princes to act,
And monarchs to behold the
swelling scene.
Then should the warlike
Harry, like himself,
Assume the port of Mars,
and at his heels,
Leashed in like hounds, should
famine, sword,
and fire
Crouch for employment.
But pardon, gentles all,
The flat unraiséd spirits that
hath dared
On this unworthy scaffold to
bring forth
So great an object. Can this
cock-pit hold
The vasty fields of France?
Or may we cram
Within this wooden O the
very casques
That did affright the air at
Agincourt?
O pardon: since a crookéd
figure may
Attest in little place a million,
And let us, ciphers to this
great account,
On your imaginary forces work.

William Shakespeare was certainly in London writing plays by 1592, because another playwright, Robert Greene, attacks him in a pamphlet. Shakespeare must have been a newish writer on the scene because Greene calls him an 'upstart crow' but, although described as merely 'in his own conceit the only Shake-scene in a country' his work must have been relatively well known for Greene makes a point of parodying a line from *Henry VI Part III*. He was almost certainly acting too, and we know he was still an actor, appearing in Ben Jonson's play *Every Man in his Humour* in 1598 and five years later in the younger playwright's *Sejanus, his Fall* for Jonson names him in the cast in the published texts. However, we do not know where or when he entered either profession, or when he wrote his first poetry.

In the Spring of 1593, his witty poem retelling the story of Venus and Adonis was published by fellow Stratfordian Richard Field, followed the next year by *The Rape of Lucrece*, both dedicated to a young nobleman, Henry Wriothesley (pronounced Wrizley), Earl of Southampton and Baron Titchfield. In 1595 Shakespeare is named as one of the members of a newly-founded company of actors known as The Lord Chamberlain's Men. By then he seems to have written a number of plays including the three parts of *Henry VI*, *Richard III*, *Titus Andronicus*, *Two Gentlemen of Verona*, *The Taming of the Shrew* and *Love's Labour's Lost*. The title page of *Titus*, published in 1594, announces it as acted by three different companies so it is probable that he had not previously committed himself to any one group of players.

He had shown that he could write plays that suited performance conditions and were popular with audiences. We can surmise that by then he had proved himself a competent actor, if not a great one. There is a tradition, going back perhaps to the reports of those who knew him, that he had a liking for 'kingly' parts and also played such roles as the old man Adam in *As You Like It* and the Ghost in *Hamlet*. He also seems to have found favour and patronage in fashionable circles.

Henry Wriothesley, barely 20 years old when *Venus and Adonis* was dedicated to him, was already known for his interest in and patronage of poets. He was a good-looking young man, wore his hair in long curls that were not yet in fashion, was wealthy and in favour with the Queen. When eight years old, on his father's death, he was made a ward of court and placed under the care of the Lord Treasurer, William Cecil, Lord Burleigh. Sent to Cambridge at 12 years old, he gained his Master of Arts degree at 16 and went to Gray's Inn to complete his education. He wished to emulate the Queen's favourite, the Earl of Essex, (in 1601 he was to go to the Tower for supporting the Essex rebellion against Elizabeth) and to join him in a military expedition rather than stay at home, marry and produce an heir as his mother and Lord Burghley were eager that he should do.

It is possible that his mother and Burghley commissioned Shakespeare to write at least some of the *Sonnets* to convince young Henry of the need to marry – though the same has been

London in 1572, a map attributed to Georg Höfnagel in *Civitates Orbis Terrarum*. The Queen's Palace of Whitehall is on the far left, the Tower of London on the right. The modern City of London is the area defined by the city wall which extends north from the Tower and across to the west, pierced by its gates, until it comes south to the river at about the centre of the map. The modern 'West End' is on the fields above the curve of the river on the left. From Whitehall Palace the road goes north to Charing Cross (St. Giles-in-the-Fields is shown in an island of roads a little further north), then sweeps along the Strand, past the church of St. Clement Dane, then along Fleet Street and Ludgate Hill to curve around Old St. Paul's and on as Cheapside, Poultry and Eastcheap towards the Tower. From St. Giles, Holborn runs east to Smithfield, the open market place, north of which Clerkenwell is named, while to the northeast, close by the arms of the city, is Spitalfields.

This is very much the London which Shakespeare first knew, although even then it was expanding. James Burbage built his Theatre in Shoreditch, a little further out than Spitalfields along the road going north from Bishopsgate, and nearby, the Curtain was also erected. South of the river, above the heads of the two women, are two circular buildings used for bull- and bear-baiting. This is the area where Shakespeare's Globe theatre was to stand.

Despite the destruction of the Great Fire of 1666 and four centuries of expansion and rebuilding, much of the original pattern still remains and modern street names still bear witness to the old London which has disappeared.

suggested of the Countess of Pembroke, in which case they would have been directed at *her* son. Shakespeare's dedication of *The Rape of Lucrece* is much more personal than that of his first volumes and suggests a certain intimacy between them. If the *Sonnets* were written at this time, and that is not certain (they did not appear in print until 1609, although they had been in private circulation for some time and two had appeared in another collection in 1599)

Southampton would appear to fit the unknown person to whom they are addressed. The published dedication to their 'only begetter Mr W.H.' was made by the printer and could have a quite different meaning; scholars' arguments identifying the initials as William Herbert (Pembroke, aged 14 in 1594) or as a coded reversal of Henry Wriothesley may therefore be irrelevant.

The declarations of love in the Sonnets and the 'love without end' may

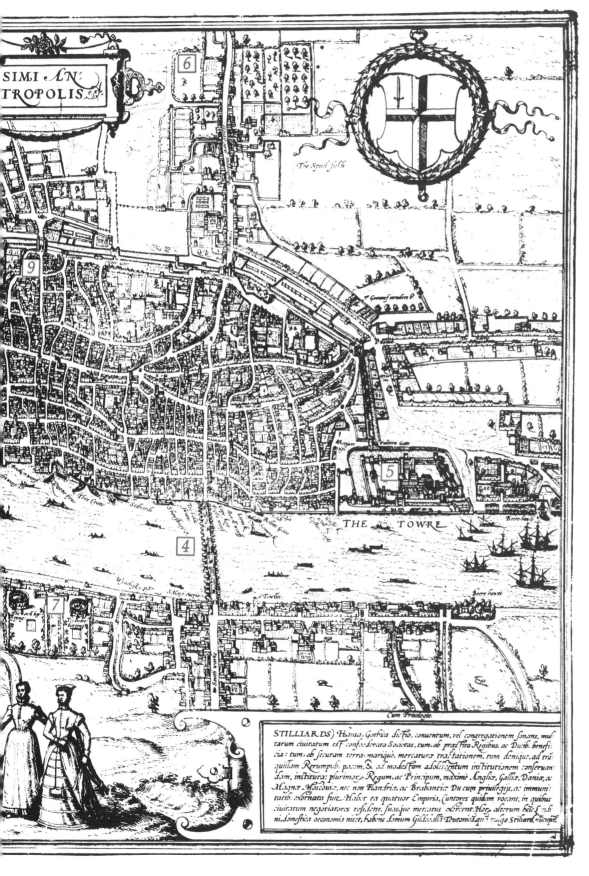

KEY

1. Westminster Abbey. The boys of Westminster School acted in Latin plays.
2. Palace of Whitehall.
3. St. Paul's Cathedral.
4. London Bridge.
5. The Tower of London.
6. The first theatres were built near here.
7. Bankside, the pleasure area where later theatres were built.
8. Middle Temple, one of the Inns of Court where plays were performed.
9. Shakespeare's lodging on the corner of Mugle Street and Silver Street.
10. Blackfriars, where the old hall was turned into a private theatre and Shakespeare bought a house.

Titchfield Abbey, Hampshire, country seat of Henry Wriothesley, Earl of Southampton. He was Shakespeare's patron and there are some who think that the *Sonnets* may have been dedicated to him. Shakespeare may well have lived for a time in his London house in Holborn and come to Hampshire at times when he was not needed in London or when theatres were closed because of plague.

FAR RIGHT
The Hall of Middle Temple, Inns of Court. The students at the Inns of Court were not all destined to be lawyers; young gentleman were sent here as to a kind of finishing-school to learn manners as well as jurisprudence, Shakespeare's patron, the young Earl of Southampton being among them. Like the students at the universities, they staged amateur performances of plays, but they also invited professional companies of players to entertain them and their guests. The end screen and gallery would have supplied the actors with entrances and an upper level when needed for special scenes or for musicians. *Twelfth Night* was presented here on 2 February 1602. One lawyer, John Massingham recorded in his diary: 'At our feast wee had a play called Twelve Night or What you Will, much like the Comedy of Errores.' Certainly, both plays use the convention of siblings being mistaken for each other, but one cannot help but wonder how far Massingham must have been in his cups to have found *Twelfth Night* so similar to *The Comedy of Errors*.

reflect the fulsomeness of Elizabethan hyperbole and courtly style rather than homoerotic attraction but the outpouring of feeling to 'my lovely boy' is without equal. If not fictitious this was a deeply-felt attachment, sharpened by the behaviour of the 'dark lady' with whom they both became involved. The *Sonnets* may not have been meant for Southampton, but even without them his patronage seems rather more involving than a mere dedication might suggest.

In 1592 there was a serious out-

Things got so bad for The Earl of Pembroke's Men that they were forced to sell their costumes. Consequently, they would not have been eager to buy new plays and this could account for Shakespeare turning to narrative verse. It is possible that he actually became part of Southampton's household, or a

break of plague in London and from June that year through to May of 1594 the theatres were not able to open. Prevented from earning their living in the city, actors were forced to go on tour in the provinces or abroad, or find some other way to support themselves.

guest at his London mansion, South-ampton House in Holborn, and his Hampshire home, Titchfield Abbey in Hampshire. It has also been suggested that the Italian setting of *Two Gentlemen of Verona, Romeo and Juliet* and *The Merchant of Venice,* which were probably the next plays to be written, indicate that Shakespeare made a trip to Italy, perhaps with Southampton.

When the worst fears of plague retreated, a new grouping of actors, including Richard Burbage, a fine tragedian, William Kemp, dancer and comedian, and William Shakespeare, formed a company under the patronage of Henry Carey, Lord Hunsdon who was Lord Chamberlain: they called themselves The Chamberlain's Men. Although independent commercial companies, the patronage of a peer gave a band of actors a token attachment to his household and as his 'servants' protected them from prosecution under laws governing vagabonds and beggars. The Chamberlain's Men performed at a playhouse called The Theatre, which Burbage's father had built in 1576 at Shoreditch, a rapidly growing suburb outside the city walls. Like all the acting companies they consisted of a number of shareholders who ran the company (and were often the leading actors) and hired men which included actors, musicians and back stage help, as well as boy actors who played the female and children's roles. The boys were probably apprenticed to the adult actors who would pass on skills to them. There were no actresses on the professional stage in England until half a century after Shakespeare's death, when they were introduced during the reign of Charles II.

The Theatre was London's first purpose-built playhouse. It was outside the walls to escape the jurisdiction of the City Fathers, many of whom disapproved of plays on moral and religious grounds. They were also concerned that they might be a threat to public order, that the audience might riot and such crowds increase the risk of spreading the plague. The law forbade performances within the City without their express permission.

The Theatre's success led to the building in 1577 of a rival, the Curtain, close by but nearer to the City, the better to steal the audience. These playhouses were circular or polygonal buildings with galleries surrounding a space open to the sky, like the inn yards in which actors had often played, with a platform projecting into it. There was no stage lighting: plays were performed in day time, night scenes indicated in the dialogue or by lanterns and candles. There was no attempt at scenic illusion, though items such as a tree with apples to pick were among stage furniture along with thrones and beds – words and token properties set the scene, helped by costumes, music and sound effects.

Within the City the Choir Masters at the Chapel Royal and St. Paul's also converted existing buildings into indoor theatres where the boys of their choir

OPPOSITE
The George Inn, Southwark. The galleries of this London Inn, not far from Bankside, would once have ranged round at least three sides of a yard and such places, offering clear sightlines for many spectators on the upper levels, were ideal for travelling players to put on a show. They greatly influenced the design of the first English theatre buildings.

A copy, made from a drawing in the commonplace book of Arend van Buchel of Utrect, itself a copy of a sketch which his friend Johannes de Witt made on a visit to London in or about 1596. It shows the Swan Theatre, on Bankside, and is the only known contemporary picture of an Elizabethan playhouse.

schools performed plays for a more exclusive, 'private' audience.

In 1587, another playhouse called the Rose, opened south of the Thames on Bankside, west of London Bridge, which was already an area of brothels and entertainments, including the brutal sports of bear- and bull-baiting.

The Chamberlain's Men were popular, not just with the playhouse audiences but for performances at Court and other special bookings. Their chief rivals were The Admiral's Men at the Rose, led by Edward Alleyn, like Burbage a fine actor and one who, on several visits to Stratford, may well have fired young Shakespeare with an enthusiasm for the stage.

The land on which The Theatre was built was only leased and when this expired in 1597 there was difficulty with the landlord. From then until some time in 1599, The Chamberlain's Men played mainly at the Curtain in which the Burbage family now had a share, though it was not in a good state of repair.

Meanwhile, in 1596, another playhouse, the Swan (see sketch on page 53) had been built on Bankside by Francis Langley, a friend of Shakespeare's. They had been accused together of threatening a corrupt Southwark magistrate. The Chamberlain's Men could perhaps have transferred there but unfortunately, in July 1597, *The Isle of Dogs,* a play by Ben Jonson and Thomas Nashe presented at the Swan had so enraged the authorities that the Privy Council put Jonson and the actors in prison (Nashe managed to avoid arrest) and ordered that all theatres be pulled down. That order was never carried out but they still refused to let Langley put plays on at the Swan. The Burbages (Burbage Senior had died that year) had also acquired the hall at Blackfriars used by the choir school boy actors, but the Privy Council would not give that a licence either.

Shakespeare and his fellows took desperate measures. They signed a

lease for a site close by the Rose. It would be their's from Christmas Day 1598. On 26 December they were acting before the Queen at Whitehall Palace. Two days later, while their Shoreditch landlord and the rest of London were still busy celebrating Christmas they pulled down The Theatre and transported its timbers across the river to Bankside to build a new theatre – the Globe. The Burbages did not want to bear the whole cost and several actors put up money and became shareholders in the theatre as well as the acting company. Shakespeare had one tenth.

Elizabeth I died in 1603 and the new king, James I (James VI of Scotland) became the company's patron. They

Wilton House, near Salisbury, Wiltshire, country home of William Herbert, the young Earl of Pembroke, another possible person to whom the *Sonnets* may have been dedicated and patron of a company of actors. According to a letter written by Lady Pembroke to her son, now lost but claimed to have been in the family archives, young William was requested to bring King James I to visit early in December 1603 because 'we have the man Shakespeare with us'. On 2 December, The King's Men are believed to have performed *As You Like It* for him. The central part is all that remains of the Tudor house; the wings were designed by Inigo Jones in 1648 after a fire had destroyed the rest.

changed their name to The King's Men and the main shareholders were given the honorary posts of Grooms of the Royal Bedchamber. But plague hit London, the theatres were closed and The King's Men went on tour. It was at Wilton House, near Salisbury, that they first acted before the King and it was March 1604 when James finally made his state progress through London – the Grooms were each granted four and a half yards of scarlet cloth for their liveries. Only then could the theatres open again. The new king liked plays even more than Queen Elizabeth and The King's Men were often to appear before him.

Shakespeare was then lodging in the

BELOW
The Church of St. Mary Overy, now Southwark Cathedral, stands at the foot of London Bridge and close to Bankside where London theatre and entertainment was concentrated at the end of the 16th century. It became the actors' church and here Shakespeare buried his brother Edmund in 1607. He too had been an actor, though not a member of the same company. The view on pages 60-61 was sketched from the cathedral's tower.

house of Christopher Mountjoy, a maker of ladies' headdresses, near Cripplegate, a solidly respectable neighbourhood near Neville's Inn and the Barber-Surgeon's Hall. He had previously lived somewhere near Bishopsgate, where he was being chased for taxes in 1597. But that same year he became much involved with buying a fine house at Stratford-upon-Avon which he must have thought of as his permanent home. There is no record of

OPPOSITE
The Swan Theatre, Stratford-upon-Avon, opened in 1986. This modern theatre, echoing the Elizabethan playhouse in form, was built within the shell of the old Shakespeare Memorial Theatre, burned down in 1926. Though neither its design nor its productions attempt historical reconstruction of Elizabethan style, it manages to create a great feeling of warmth and intimacy between actor and audience.

Shakespeare owning property in London until 1613, when he paid £140 for the gatehouse of the old Blackfriars Priory, on St. Andrew's Hill, convenient for the 'private' theatre. This was probably bought more for investment than as a home for, though he still made visits to London, his life was now becoming more centred on Stratford.

In 1608 the company moved into the Blackfriars candlelit 'private' theatre, which probably made it easier to create the magical effects for *The Tempest*. Such later plays probably consciously catered to the taste of its smaller, exclusive audience. Here they could ignore the weather and play through the winter but their main audience was still on Bankside and the Globe remained Shakespeare's main playhouse until,

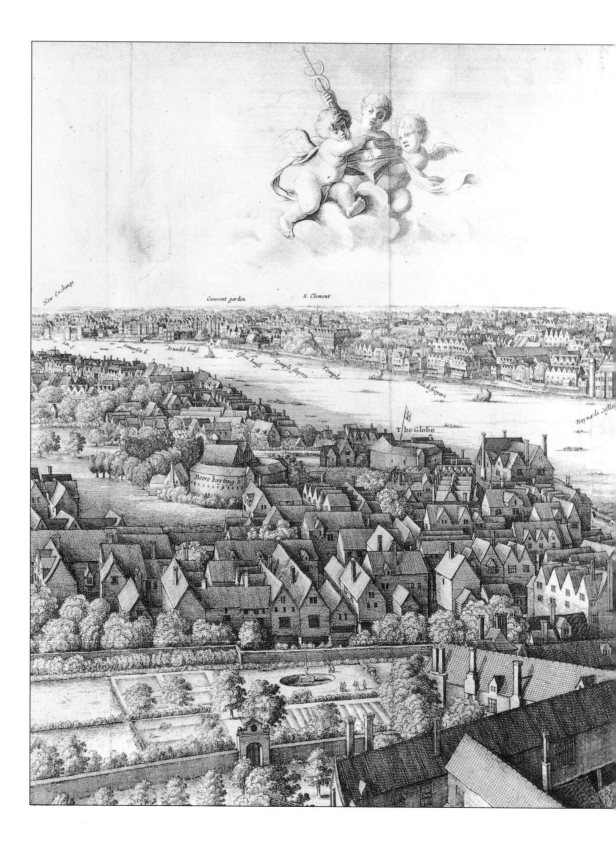

during a performance of *Henry VIII* in June 1613, a mishandled cannon effect set fire to the thatch roof and it burned down. A new Globe was build as soon as possible, but it was the old theatre that had seen the premières of *Hamlet* and most of the great later plays – he is not known to have written anything for the new theatre. Perhaps his health was poor in London and he decided to retire to Stratford. Perhaps he felt the destruction of the Globe signalled the time to let others shoulder the burden: after all, in about 22 years he had written nearly four-score plays, as well as sonnets and long poems. He had also been involved with acting and running the company. He had earned a rest and could afford to take it.

Part of a panorama of London engraved by Wenzel Hollar and published in Amsterdam in 1647. It shows the second Globe Theatre, which was demolished in 1644. Hollar, who had been forced to leave England earlier that year, had already made the drawings (which still exist) from which he worked, sketching from the tower of Southwark Cathedral. Back in Antwerp, when he came to add the labels, his memory failed him and he somehow switched those of the 'Globe' and 'Beere bayting'. The Globe playhouse is on the left with a double gable over the stage canopy and a cupola. Just above St. George's flag flying from the other building you can see the label 'Blackfreyars' where Shakespeare bought a house. Blackfriar's Hall, turned into a 'private' theatre for which some of Shakespeare's later plays were written, is probably the building with the very long roof a little to the right of this.

STRATFORD: MAN OF PROPERTY

The foundations and cellarage are all that can be seen today of Shakespeare's fine house, New Place. The only known drawing of it, and that made from memory by George Vertue some 30 years after it had been pulled down, shows the Chapel Street frontage as two-storeyed with dormer-windowed attics or a gabled third floor spread over five bays, with an imposing central entrance porch.

While William found success in London, Anne and the children stayed in Stratford, presumably living at Henley Street with his parents. John Shakespeare, when he was Bailiff and before the setback in his fortunes, had applied to the College of Arms for a grant of armorial bearings. In 1596 the claim was again pursued, for to add to John's own former civic status and his wife's Arden heritage he now had a son with connections in high places. In October a draft design was prepared by Garter King of Arms. But for William that summer brought tragedy. Early in August his son

Hamnet died, aged only eleven-and-a-half. There is no record of whether it was illness or accident but there was now no son to inherit the arms and rank of a gentleman, and though Anne, aged 40, was not necessarily past child-bearing there were to be no more children. Indeed, William's brothers were also to die, unmarried and childless, before him, leaving no male line to succeed.

There had been two disastrous fires in Stratford, more than 200 buildings had been destroyed and part of Henley Street pulled down to stop the flames from spreading. There was rebuilding in

Stratford and with funds available Shakespeare decided to move his wife and daughters from his parents' house, where his grown up brothers and sisters Gilbert, Joan, Anne, Richard and 16-year-old Edmund were also living.

In May, William bought one of the finest houses in Stratford town, New Place, just across Chapel Lane from the Gild Chapel and grammar school, which had been built for Sir Hugh Clopton in the 1490s and was the first house in Stratford to be built with timber and brick rather than wattle and daub. It had been rescued from dilapidation by a local landowner who was a Temple lawyer when Shakespeare was a boy and it now made a fine home for a newly-created gentleman. With a main frontage of 60ft (18m) and a depth of 70ft (21m) it was the second largest house in Stratford, had ten fireplaces – so presumably at least ten rooms – two barns, orchards and gardens. It cost

Shakespeare £60. He very likely made some repairs and alterations for, next year, he is credited with selling a quantity of stone to the borough, surplus no doubt to his requirements or the result of pulling down some outbuildings. It is possible that Shakespeare now spent more time at Stratford, concentrating on writing new plays instead of touring with The Chamberlain's Men as an actor, and it seems he kept an eye open for local business opportunities.

The barns were soon put to good use for housing grain — he is listed by the council in 1598 as having a store of corn and malt. This may have been to ensure stocks for the family at a time of shortage when many in the country were starving or it may have been put aside to sell at high prices due to its scarcity. Profits made in London were probably mainly invested in property.

In the Spring of 1602, Shakespeare purchased 127 acres of agricultural

A striking display of topiary in the gardens of New Place.

The gardens of Shakespeare's house, New Place, have been planted to suggest the Elizabethan style. Here Shakespeare is said to have planted a mulberry tree. There is one there today, not the same one, but perhaps one of its descendants. The first tree was cut down by the then owner the Reverend Francis Gastrell because so many people came to his door asking to look at it. (That was only the beginning: six years after buying New Place he had the house demolished.) In 1759, he sold the tree to a Stratford watchmaker who used it to make souvenirs, so many, in fact, that it would seem that the tree must have magically multiplied itself. The second tree was claimed to have been from a cutting from the original tree. That was blown down in August 1946 and its replacement came from a nursery of cuttings which the Birthplace Trust (who own the property) had been keeping as an insurance against such a calamity.

64

Perhaps Shakespeare was himself fond of gardening. He certainly understood some of the basics of horticulture when he made this analogy between good husbandry and the care of the kingdom.

GARDENER

Go bind thou up yon dangling
apricots,
Which, like unruly children,
make their sire
Stoop with oppression of their
prodigal weight.
Give some supportance to the
bending twigs.
Go thou, and, like an
executioner,
Cut off the heads of too fast-
growing sprays
That look too lofty in our
commonwealth.
All must be even in our
government.
You thus employed, I will root
away
The noisome weeds, that
without profit suck
The soil's fertility from
wholesome flowers.

SERVANT

Why should we, in the compass
of a pale,
Keep law, and form, and due
proportion,
Showing, as in a model, our
firm estate?
When our sea-walled garden,
the whole land,
Is full of weeds, her fairest
flowers choked up,
Her fruit trees all unpruned,
her hedges ruined,
Her knots disordered, and her
wholesome herbs
Swarming with caterpillars?

Richard II Act III, Scene 4

*There is a willow grows
aslant a brook
That shows his hoar leaves
in the glassy stream.
Therewith fantastic
garlands did she make
Of crow-flowers,
nettles, daisies, and long
purples,
That liberal shepherds give
a grosser name,
But our cold maids do dead
men's fingers call them:
There on the pendent
boughs her coronet weeds
Clamb'ring to hang, an
envious sliver broke;
When down her weedy
trophies, and herself,
Fell in the weeping brook...*

Hamlet Act 4, Scene 7

In 1596 Shakespeare's only son Hamnet died. Years before, when Shakespeare was a boy, a Stratford girl called Kate Hamnet had drowned herself in the Avon. Could he have been remembering them both as he wrote the lines in which Gertrude describes the death of Ophelia in *Hamlet* (above).

OPPOSITE
The scenes of sheep-shearing merry-making in *A Winter's Tale*, one of Shakespeare's last plays, evoke bucolic Warwickshire and here, as Perdita gives flowers to her guests, he displays his feeling for the flowers of both countryside and garden.

... daffodils,
That come before the swallow dares, and take
The winds of March with beauty; violets, dim,
But sweeter than the lids of Juno's eyes
Or Cytherea's breath; pale primroses,
That die unmarried ere they can behold
Bright Phoebus in his strength, a malady
Most incident to maids; bold oxlips, and
The crown-imperial; lilies of all kinds,
The flower-de-luce being one...

The Winter's Tale Act 4, Scene 3

The Welcombe Hills, just outside Stratford on the Warwick road. Shakespeare owned a lease of tithes near here and opposed the wishes of the Combe family to enclose the land in 1614-15.

Dover's Hill, between Broadway and Chipping Camden. Here, in the early years of the 17th century, Robert Dover inaugurated the Whitsun-Ale Games, or, perhaps more likely, revived an earlier Cotswold custom. Held on the Tuesday of Whitsun Week, they included wrestling, dancing, horseraces, and shin-kicking! Disapproved of by the Puritans, they attracted the support of the local gentry, including that of courtier and friend of poets and artists, Endymion Porter. One year he acquired some cast-off clothes from King James and Dover sported the royal plumed hat. Porter published a book, *Annalia Dubrensia*, to which Ben Jonson, John Heywood and Michael Drayton contributed celebratory verses. If the event was already a feature of the 1590s, before Dover drew attention to it, then there may be some truth in the suggestion that it gave Shakespeare the idea for the wrestling match in *As You Like It*. In 1850, the Vicar of Weston-under-Edge campaigned against the rowdiness and immoral influence of the Games upon his parisioners and, in 1851, the land was enclosed and the custom ended though it has been revived again in recent years.

land in Old Stratford, north of the town: this was a considerable investment of £320. He must have been in London when the deal was settled for the negotiations were done by his brother Gilbert.

In September he bought a cottage in Chapel Lane, perhaps it was needed to house a gardener or domestic staff, but it made another addition to his property portfolio. At some time in or before 1604 he also acquired another cottage and garden in Rowington Manor. Then in 1606 he paid £440 for an interest in a lease of tithes in the Stratford area (which brought him a handsome return of £60 per annum).

ABOVE
Modern Morris dancers at Stratford. Morris dances, traditionally performed by men only, probably have their origins in fertility rituals. The name, originally 'Morisco' or Moorish dance, links them with Los Matchinos of Spain and New Mexico which nominally celebrate the expulsion of the Moors from Spain in the 15th century. Dancers often assume particular characters, such as Maid Marian, or even contemporary figures, a policeman for instance in modern times. The same groups probably also performed the mummers' plays which drew their material from traditional stories such as that of St. George, and often have a strong connection with fertility ritual. Dancers usually wear bells on their legs and carry flat sticks or poles that are woven into a 'knot' at the end of the dance. Originally they were swords or knives and the knot may have held the head of a blood sacrifice.

Hall's Croft, in Stratford Old Town, was the home of Shakespeare's daughter, Susanna, after her marriage to Dr. John Hall in 1607. At least, that is the tradition, though it seems to go back only to the 19th century. It is certainly a fine example of a large house of the right period, a fitting home for a successful physician.

OPPOSITE
The garden of Hall's Croft

In September 1601, John Shakespeare died, leaving the Henley Street house to William. Sister Joan had married a hatter called William Hart soon after the purchase of New Place. They had moved into Anne and the children's rooms at Henley Street and now they stayed on there after his mother's death in 1608. A few years later, after her other brothers died, the part of the premises given over to the glove-making business was let for use as an inn.

When Shakespeare's eldest daughter Susanna married the eminently successful young doctor John Hall in 1607, only Anne and Judith were left in permanent residence at New Place.

Rooms were therefore let as lodgings to the Town Clerk, Thomas Greene, who moved into the house with his wife and two children. The arrangement was to be a limited one – they knew that they were expected to leave when Shakespeare decided to make a permanent move back to Stratford.

Susanna had a daughter Elizabeth, in 1608. Could his fondness for his little granddaughter have led to this myriad of young heroines in Shakespeare's last plays – Marina in *Pericles*, written soon after her birth, Perdita in *A Winter's Tale*, Imogen in *Cymbeline* and Miranda in *The Tempest*? He may have been in Stratford for much of 1609, for plague

The 'dispensary' at Hall's Croft displays a collection of apothecary's jars for storing herbs and other medicinal preparations. John Hall was a highly regarded practitioner who published a book about some of his cases. However, it says nothing about his father-in-law.

again closed the London theatres, but Thomas Greene was able to stay on at New Place for another year.

When Shakespeare did make that move, probably in 1613, it was to a Stratford with a harsh Puritan council under whom stage plays were banned and troupes of actors were unwelcome. But in Stratford he was a property-owning gentleman, not a vagabond player. Half a century later the Rev. John Ward, the local Vicar, heard that Shakespeare 'spent at the rate of a thousand pounds a year'. His careful investments and surviving references to litigation make it difficult to imagine him squandering a penny so this probably reflects the awe with which many locals viewed his considerable wealth.

That summer of 1613 brought with it a scandal to overcome. A malicious local tradesman had spread a rumour that Mrs. Hall not only 'ran the raines' ('wore the trousers' would be the phrase today) at home but had committed adultery with a man called Rafe Smith. Susanna took out a writ against the tradesman. He failed to appear in court and she and the Shakespeare honour were vindicated.

There were still trips to London. Perhaps Shakespeare was there for the opening of the new Globe Theatre in the Spring of 1614. He was there in November with John Hall, for John Greene (Thomas' brother) saw him there about the plans to enclose some of his tithe land at Welcombe. Though it could have been to his advantage, Shakespeare voiced his disapproval.

As 1616 began, Shakespeare would have been pleased that his daughter

Not far from Shakespeare's New Place, and on the other side of the road in the High Street, was the home of the wealthy bailiff Thomas Rogers. It was built in 1596 after the previous properties had been burned down. From here he took his daughter, Katherine, to Holy Trinity for her marriage to Robert Harvard of Southwark. If Shakespeare was not in Stratford as one of the guests then he would almost certainly have been a visitor to their London home on Bankside, where, two years later, their son John was born – the founder of Harvard University. The house was presented to the University in 1909 and is now known as Harvard House.

Judith, still a spinster at 30, was to marry Thomas Quiney, son of his late friend Richard, a vintner and Stratford worthy. He drafted a will providing for both his daughters. Then there was a hiccup. The marriage was by special licence – a reminder, perhaps, of his own situation thirty-two winters earlier. There arose some irregularity and when, after the wedding, Thomas failed to turn up when summoned to a Church court at Worcester, he was excommunicated for non-attendance. Then the truth came out. Richard had got another girl with child, delivered less than a month after his wedding, when both mother and baby died. Richard was put on trial, confessed all and was ordered to make public penance.

This was not the kind of thing with which a respectable gentleman such as Shakespeare wished to be associated. Thomas, in fact, did turn out to be rather a bad lot, but this was already too much for Shakespeare, who changed his will, thereby reducing Judith's expectations. However, she was still to get her dowry of £100, the cottage in Chapel Lane, (or another £50 if she were to forgo it) and, provided that she or her children were surviving three years later, the interest on a further capital sum of £150.

Anne was to stay in her home by right, that went without saying, but Shakespeare did specify that his wife should have 'the second best bed', one way of ensuring that she kept the room she wanted. Susanna got New Place, the houses in Henley Street and Blackfriars and all other 'lands and tenementes and hereditamentes whatsoever'. These were to pass in turn to her eldest son (there was still plenty of time for her to have sons, if not to her husband), and then in entail to sons of Judith. There were minor benefactions too, including 26 shillings and eight pence each to the remaining members of the original Chamberlain's Men of

OPPOSITE
Bidford-on-Avon, downstream from Stratford and Welford, developed where the ancient Icknield Way crosses the Avon. Local Stratford tradition has it that Shakespeare took part in a drinking competition between Stratford cronies and Bidford carousers at the Falcon Inn. He fell asleep (or passed out) under a crab-tree and woke to compose the following doggerel celebrating local village names. It is unlikely, however, that it would ever have found its way into his accepted works.

Piping Pebworth, dancing Marston,
Haunted Hillborough, hungry Grafton,
Dodging Exhall, papist Wixford,
Beggarly Broom and drunken Bidford.

Cottages near Shottery.

1595, fellow actors John Heminges, Richard Burbage and Henry Condell: with this they were to buy mourning rings.

This will was signed on 25 March. It may simply have been the marriage that prompted Shakespeare to put such affairs in order, or perhaps his brother-in-law's illness, for William Harte died mid-April. Yet Shakespeare was not an old man and one wonders whether he too had already been stricken by some malady, for less than a month later he was dead.

Reverend Ward has put on record that Shakespeare had drunk too heavily at a 'merry meeting' with Ben Jonson and Michael Drayton and 'died of a feavour there contracted'. The truth we will never know. John Hall later pub-lished a book of observations on cases he had treated. They include a cure he effected for his daughter Elizabeth but unfortunately these case notes do not begin until after Shakespeare's death.

He died on 23 April and was buried at Holy Trinity Church two days later. His grave is in a privileged place before the altar and within the sanctuary rail. The stone slab that marks it bears no name, only a few lines to ask that it be unmolested – for the custom was to remove old bones from the graves of the long forgotten and to stack them in a charnel house to make room for fresh burials. Nine years later his wife died and was laid beside him.

The parish register simply records the burial of 'Will. Shakespeare, gent.' but a monument was later placed above

OPPOSITE
The nave and chancel of Holy Trinity, the parish church where Shakespeare, his children and his grandchild were all christened, his son's funeral held, his daughters married and the poet himself buried. There is a monument to the poet on the north side of the chancel, just above his grave. Here too lie his wife Anne, daughter Susanna and her husband John Hall. John Combe's tomb is to the left of the altar. He left Shakespeare £5 in his will.

Shakespeare's grave is in a place of importance within the sanctuary of the church and just in front of the altar. The simple stone slab above it does not bear his name, only the plea:

Good friend for Jesus' sake forebeare
To digg the dust encloased heare.
Bleste be the man that spares the stones
An curst be he that moves my bones.

This was so that his bones should not be dug up and thrown into a charnel house to make way for another burial, as was long the custom. There is no mention of these lines in his will, but if he had written them or they had been put there at his request, the wish has so far been granted.

GOOD FREND FOR IESVS SAKE FORBEARE,
TO DIGG THE DVST ENCLOASED HEARE:
BLESE BE Y MAN Y SPARES HES STONES,
AND CVRST BE HE Y MOVES MY BONES.

The monument to William Shakespeare, erected on the wall of the chancel a few years after his death, is of marble inlaid with touchstone, the bust by Gheerat Janssen being of painted Cotswold stone. The family arms are displayed above. The Latin part of the inscription reads:

In judgement a Nestor,
in genius a Socrates,
in art a Virgil:
The earth covers him,
the people mourn him,
Olympus has him.

The bust has not always been coloured. It was painted in 1748 by John Hall, painted out in 1793 and coloured again by Simon Collis in 1861! The pen in his hand is replaced each year at the traditional celebration of his birthday on 23 April. This is attended by official representatives from many countries whose flags are unfurled in the streets for the procession to the church where flowers are laid.

the grave to do him honour. The likeness on it presumably had the approval of the remaining members of his family. Together with the engraving (page 7) published in the collected edition of his works, it gives us some indication of his appearance.

Susanna had no more children and her daughter Elizabeth, though married twice, died childless. Judith's three sons all died young and childless too. The closest line of descent to our own time comes from his sister Joan and William Harte. But, though the bloodline was soon broken, his work is still very much alive and the spirit of Shakespeare resides in his plays and poetry. His true memorials are not the podgy bust in Holy Trinity Church or the statue in Westminster Abbey but the magnificence of his work, which his colleagues Heminges and Condell collected and published in 1623.

While his poetry can be appreciated by the private reader, it is on the stage that his plays belong and where they continue to test actors with the challenge of great roles and to captivate audiences with fine language and great theatre, making all of us his true inheritors.

Shakespeare's work, rather than statues or monuments, are his best memorial. The National Theatre, London (top) and the Royal Shakespeare Theatre, Stratford-upon-Avon, are two theatres dedicated to his memory where the plays of the Shakespeare repertoire are regularly performed.

At the annual birthday celebrations on 23 April, the Stratford beadle leads the procession of townspeople and international and theatrical representatives past the Grammar School and Gild Chapel on their way to lay flowers on Shakespeare's grave in Holy Trinity Church.